1000 Everyday Life Hacks

PA BOOKS

Published by PA BOOKS, 2023.

1000 EVERYDAY LIFE HACKS

First edition. October 28, 2023.

ISBN: 979-8223108412

Written by PA BOOKS.

Also by PA BOOKS

Hogan's Key
Kimberly & the Five Strange Goldfishes
The Enchanted Library
The Misadventures of Pirate Pete
From Wheel To Web: 40 Remarkable Inventions
Once Upon A Sleepy Time
The Global Game - The Evolution Of Football
Strides To Success: A Beginner's Guide to Running
The ChatGPT Handbook
Climate Crossroads
1000 Everyday Life Hacks
Urban Exploration - London The Comprehensive Travel Guide

Table of Contents

Chapter 1: Morning Routine Hacks

Welcome to the first chapter of "Everyday Life Hacks: Your Guide to a More Efficient and Productive Day." Your morning routine sets the tone for the entire day. In this chapter, we'll explore 100 easy and realistic hacks to help you start your day on the right foot, ensuring a productive and stress-free morning.

1. Set Multiple Alarms: Avoid oversleeping by setting multiple alarms at 5-minute intervals.

2. Place Alarm Out of Reach: Force yourself out of bed by placing the alarm clock on the opposite side of the room.

3. Pre-Set Coffee Maker: Program your coffee maker to have a fresh pot ready as soon as you wake up.

4. Morning Playlist: Create a motivating morning playlist to get you in the right mood.

5. Natural Light Exposure: Open your curtains to let in natural light, which helps regulate your circadian rhythm.

6. Hydrate: Start your day with a glass of water to kick-start your metabolism.

7. Exercise or Stretch: Even a short workout or stretch can boost energy levels.

8. Lay out Clothes: Save time by choosing your outfit the night before.

9. Pre-Pack Lunch: Prepare your lunch or snacks in advance to grab on the way out.

10. Mindful Breathing: Practice deep breathing exercises to reduce stress and anxiety.

11. Morning Shower: A warm shower can invigorate you and wake you up.

12. No Snooze Button: Resist the urge to hit the snooze button; it disrupts your sleep cycle.

13. Use a Sunrise Alarm Clock: Mimics natural sunlight to wake you gently.

14. Plan the Day: Make a to-do list for the day to stay organized.

15. Set Goals: Identify specific goals you want to achieve during the day.

16. Prioritize Tasks: Use the Eisenhower Matrix (urgent/important) to prioritize your tasks.

17. Practice Gratitude: Write down something you're grateful for each morning.

18. Time Blocks: Allocate time blocks for specific tasks to manage your day effectively.

19. Healthy Breakfast: Start your day with a nutritious breakfast to fuel your body and mind.

20. Limit Screen Time: Avoid checking emails and social media right after waking up.

21. Visualization: Visualize your day going smoothly and successfully.

22. Positive Affirmations: Recite positive affirmations to boost your confidence.

23. No Decision Mornings: Plan your morning routine the night before to minimize decisions.

24. Set a Timer: Use a timer to keep yourself on track during each task.

25. Silence Notifications: Turn off app notifications to minimize distractions.

26. Use a Morning App: Apps like "Calm" or "Headspace" can help with mindfulness and focus.

27. Write Morning Pages: Journal your thoughts and goals for the day.

28. Morning Reading: Spend time reading something inspiring or educational.

29. Keep a Morning Journal: Track your morning routine and note what works best.

30. No Morning News: Avoid starting your day with negative news.

31. Unclutter Your Mind: Clear your mental clutter with meditation or mindfulness.

32. Stretching Routine: Incorporate a short stretching routine into your morning.

33. Morning Yoga: A quick yoga session can increase flexibility and focus.

34. Listen to Podcasts: Learn something new while getting ready.

35. Self-Care Morning: Dedicate time to self-care rituals like skincare or grooming.

36. Tidy Up: Spend a few minutes DE cluttering your living space.

37. Express Love: Hug your loved ones and tell them you care.

38. Mindful Breakfast: Eat breakfast mindfully, savouring each bite.

39. Write Morning Letters: Send a short message to a friend or family member.

40. Connect with Nature: Spend a moment outside, even if it's just on your balcony.

41. Sunrise Observation: Watch the sunrise if you have a good view.

42. Fresh Air: Open the windows to let in fresh air.

43. Morning Affirmations: Repeat positive affirmations in the mirror.

44. Plan "Me Time": Dedicate time for personal hobbies or interests.

45. Set the Coffee Table: Prepare a cosy coffee or tea corner.

46. Cold Shower: Boost alertness with a cold shower.

47. Morning Review: Reflect on the previous day and plan improvements.

48. Morning Walk: Take a brisk walk to wake up your body.

49. Mindful Eating: Pay attention to the flavours and textures of your breakfast.

50. Morning Gratitude Walk: Walk while listing things you're grateful for.

51. Aromatherapy: Use essential oils for a calming or invigorating aroma.

52. No Phone Zone: Create a "no phone" zone for your morning routine.

53. Practice Minimalism: Simplify your morning routine by having fewer items.

54. Warm Beverage: Enjoy a warm beverage like herbal tea or warm water with lemon.

55. Morning Affirmation Cards: Use cards with positive affirmations.

56. DE clutter Your Digital Space: Clear your email inbox and desktop.

57. Mindful Commute: Practice mindfulness while commuting.

58. Morning Devotion: Start the day with prayer or meditation.

59. Time for Family: Spend quality time with your family or pets.

60. Gratitude Journal: Write down three things you're grateful for.

61. Morning Rituals for Kids: Establish positive routines for children.

62. Fresh Flowers: Keep fresh flowers in your home for a cheerful morning.

63. Inspiring Quotes: Post inspirational quotes where you can see them.

64. Morning Art: Engage in creative activities like drawing or painting.

65. Prepare a Smoothie: Make a healthy morning smoothie.

66. Morning Stretches for Kids: Teach children simple stretches.

67. Mindful Breathing for Kids: Teach kids to calm down with deep breaths.

68. Morning Dance Party: Dance to your favourite music.

69. Morning Scents for Kids: Use kid-friendly essential oils.

70. Empowering Morning Mantras: Create mantras that empower you.

71. Morning Self-Care for Kids: Teach children basic grooming habits.

72. Morning Hugs and Kisses: Exchange affection with your family.

73. Morning Mindfulness for Kids: Teach kids about mindfulness.

74. Work Out with a Friend: Exercise with a buddy to stay motivated.

75. Morning Playtime: Enjoy a quick play session with your pets.

76. Mindful Breathing for Couples: Share a calming breath exercise with your partner.

77. Morning Kiss: Start your day with a kiss for your significant other.

78. Morning Play with Babies: Engage in gentle play with infants.

79. Creative Breakfast Ideas: Try new, creative breakfast recipes.

80. Morning Planning with Kids: Involve children in planning the day.

81. Morning Snuggles: Share cosy moments with your family.

82. Morning Jokes: Start your day with laughter by sharing jokes.

83. Morning Goal Setting with Kids: Teach goal setting to children.

84. Morning Affirmations for Couples: Share affirmations with your partner.

85. Morning Love Letters: Leave love notes for your partner.

86. Morning Art with Kids: Create art together.

87. Morning Affirmations for Families: Recite affirmations as a family.

88. Morning Dance Party with Kids: Have a dance party with children.

89. Morning Nature Walk: Connect with nature in the morning.

90. Morning Self-Care for Couples: Groom together.

91. Mindful Breathing for Families: Practice deep breaths as a family.

92. Morning Goals with Couples: Set goals together.

93. Morning Meditation with Kids: Teach kids meditation techniques.

94. Morning Yoga with Couples: Do couples' yoga to connect.

95. Morning Gratitude Circle: Share what you're grateful for as a family.

96. Morning Encouragement for Kids: Offer words of encouragement.

97. Morning Nature Observation with Kids: Explore nature together.

98. Morning Creative Writing: Write morning affirmations or a journal.

99. Morning Act of Kindness: Perform a small act of kindness for someone.

100. Set a Weekly Morning Ritual: Design a unique morning ritual for each day of the week.

Chapter 2: Productivity Hacks

Welcome to the second chapter of "Everyday Life Hacks: Your Guide to a More Efficient and Productive Day." In this chapter, we'll explore 100 easy and realistic productivity hacks to help you make the most of your time, stay organized, and accomplish your goals. These hacks will empower you to boost your efficiency and effectiveness in various aspects of your life.

1. Prioritize Tasks: Start your day by identifying your most important tasks and tackle them first.

2. The Two-Minute Rule: If a task can be completed in two minutes or less, do it immediately.

3. Time Blocking: Allocate specific blocks of time for different tasks to stay focused.

4. Pomodoro Technique: Work in 25-minute intervals with a 5-minute break in between.

5. Eliminate Distractions: Turn off notifications and set specific times for email and social media.

6. Use To-Do Lists: Keep a list of tasks and goals to guide your daily activities.

7. One-Minute Rule: If a task takes less than a minute, do it right away.

8. Create a Morning Routine: Establish a structured start to your day for consistency.

9. Set SMART Goals: Make your goals Specific, Measurable, Achievable, Relevant, and Time-bound.

10. Break Big Tasks into Smaller Steps: Divide complex tasks into manageable sub-tasks.

11. Use the Eisenhower Matrix: Categorize tasks as urgent/important, and prioritize accordingly.

12. Batch Similar Tasks: Group similar tasks to minimize mental switching.

13. Delegate Where Possible: Assign tasks to others when appropriate.

14. Time-Saving Apps: Utilize productivity apps for task management and time tracking.

15. Mind Mapping: Use mind maps to visualize ideas and organize thoughts.

16. Weekly Planning: Set aside time each week to plan the upcoming week.

17. Use Keyboard Shortcuts: Learn and use keyboard shortcuts to save time on your computer.

18. Auto-Text Expansions: Create shortcuts for frequently used phrases or email responses.

19. DE clutter Your Workspace: A clean workspace enhances focus and productivity.

20. Task Automation: Automate repetitive tasks using tools like Zapier or IFTTT.

21. Optimize Your Email: Organize your inbox with folders, filters, and unsubscribe from unnecessary emails.

22. Eliminate Decision Fatigue: Reduce the number of decisions you need to make by planning ahead.

23. Set Daily Intentions: Decide on your primary focus for the day.

24. Set a Timer: Use the Pomodoro Technique or other time management methods to allocate focused work intervals.

25. Time Tracking: Track how you spend your time to identify areas for improvement.

26. Take Breaks: Regular short breaks can refresh your mind and boost productivity.

27. Use a Whiteboard: Visualize tasks and deadlines on a whiteboard for easy reference.

28. Use a Planner: Organize your tasks, appointments, and goals in a physical or digital planner.

29. Outsource Tasks: Delegate personal or professional tasks to free up time.

30. Set Deadlines: Give yourself deadlines even for tasks that don't have external time constraints.

31. Zero Notifications Day: Designate one day a week without any notifications.

32. Monthly Goals: Set monthly goals to track your progress and achievements.

33. Learn to Say No: Avoid overcommitting by politely declining tasks or events.

34. Minimize Meetings: Only schedule meetings when necessary and keep them brief.

35. Email Filters and Folders: Organize your emails with filters and folders for easier access.

36. Batch Email Checking: Set specific times for checking and responding to emails.

37. Consolidate Errands: Combine multiple errands into one trip to save time.

38. Use the 2-Minute Rule: If it takes two minutes or less, do it right away.

39. Habit Stacking: Pair a new habit with an existing one to create a routine.

40. Block off Focus Time: Reserve time in your schedule for uninterrupted, focused work.

41. Limit Multitasking: Focus on one task at a time to enhance productivity.

42. The "Five Whys" Technique: Ask "why" five times to get to the root cause of a problem.

43. Use a Password Manager: Save time and enhance security with a password manager.

44. Clear Desktop Clutter: Organize and DE clutter your computer desktop for a clear workspace.

45. Inbox Zero: Aim to clear your email inbox daily or weekly.

46. Use a Second Monitor: Enhance productivity with dual screens for multitasking.

47. DE clutter Digital Files: Organize and delete unnecessary files and documents.

48. Automate Bill Payments: Set up automatic payments for bills to save time.

49. Limit Decision Fatigue: Simplify daily decisions by having a routine for meals and clothing.

50. Mindful Eating: Take breaks and savour your food for a productive lunch break.

51. Minimize Notifications: Turn off non-essential app notifications on your phone.

52. Outsource Personal Tasks: Hire services for home cleaning, grocery shopping, etc.

53. Power Naps: A short nap during the day can recharge your energy and focus.

54. Optimize Your Smartphone: Organize apps, clear cache, and update regularly.

55. Keep a Notebook: Jot down ideas, tasks, and notes to DE clutter your mind.

56. Use Checklists: Create checklists for recurring tasks to streamline execution.

57. Batch Social Media: Schedule social media posts in advance.

58. Prioritize Self-Care: Make self-care a daily routine to boost productivity.

59. Set Communication Hours: Specify hours for phone calls and meetings to avoid interruptions.

60. Visualize Your Goals: Create a vision board to remind yourself of your goals.

61. Try Time Tracking Apps: Use apps like Toggl to track how you spend your time.

62. Digital Detox: Take a day or weekend to disconnect from digital devices.

63. Prioritize Sleep: Ensure you get enough rest to be productive during the day.

64. Quick Delegation: Teach family members to handle certain household tasks.

65. Optimize Browser Tabs: Limit the number of open browser tabs for better focus.

66. Voice Notes: Use voice memos or apps to record ideas and reminders.

67. Set Realistic Goals: Don't overcommit; set achievable goals for the day.

68. Personalized Rewards: Reward yourself after completing tasks.

69. Dress for Success: Dress comfortably yet professionally to boost your confidence.

70. Proactive Problem Solving: Address problems immediately instead of procrastinating.

71. Regular Physical Activity: Exercise boosts energy and focus.

72. Short Stand-Up Meetings: Keep team meetings concise and on-topic.

73. Avoid Rush Hour Commutes: Adjust your schedule to avoid heavy traffic.

74. Email Templates: Create templates for recurring email responses.

75. Clear Physical Clutter: Regularly DE clutter you're living and working spaces.

76. Habit Tracking Apps: Use apps to monitor your progress in building positive habits.

77. Effective Email Signatures: Customize your email signature with important details.

78. Positive Affirmations: Recite positive affirmations to maintain a productive mind-set.

79. Use the "Two-Do" Technique: Choose the two most important tasks for the day.

80. Digital Note-Taking: Use digital apps for note-taking and organization.

81. Daily Reflection: Reflect on your accomplishments and areas for improvement.

82. The ABCD Priority System: Prioritize tasks using an ABCD system based on importance.

83. Automated Bill Pay: Set up automatic bill payments to avoid late fees.

84. Recurring Reminders: Use reminders for repetitive tasks and appointments.

85. Master Task Lists: Maintain a master task list for all your projects.

86. Digital Meeting Notes: Use digital apps for taking meeting notes.

87. Eliminate Unnecessary Apps: Regularly review and delete unused apps.

88. The 10-Minute Tidy: Dedicate ten minutes to tidy up your workspace daily.

89. Break for Mindfulness: Take a few minutes for deep breathing and mindfulness exercises.

90. No Unplanned Overtime: Avoid working overtime without a set plan.

91. Limit Social Media Time: Set a specific time limit for social media use.

92. Project Breakdowns: Break down complex projects into smaller tasks.

93. Backup Files: Regularly backup important digital files to prevent data loss.

94. DND Hours: Designate specific "Do Not Disturb" hours for deep work.

95. Centralized Charging Station: Create a dedicated charging station for devices.

96. Personalized Habit Tracker: Design your habit tracker to align with your goals.

97. The Power of No: Politely decline tasks or commitments that don't align with your goals.

98. Mindful Filing: Keep a clutter-free digital and physical filing system.

99. Offline Reading List: Create a list of articles and books to read during downtime.

100. Reflect and Adjust: Regularly review and adjust your productivity strategies to improve continuously.

Chapter 3: Health and Fitness Hacks

Welcome to the third chapter of "Everyday Life Hacks: Your Guide to a Healthier You." In this chapter, we'll explore 100 easy and realistic health and fitness hacks to help you prioritize your well-being. These hacks cover a wide range of areas, from exercise and nutrition to mental health and self-care, ensuring you have the tools to lead a healthier and more fulfilling life.

1. Hydrate: Start your day with a glass of water to kick-start your metabolism.

2. Portion Control: Use smaller plates to help control portion sizes.

3. Balanced Breakfast: Ensure your breakfast includes protein, fibre, and healthy fats.

4. Meal Prep: Prepare healthy meals in advance to avoid unhealthy food choices.

5. Mindful Eating: Eat slowly and savour each bite to prevent overeating.

6. Plan Your Meals: Create a weekly meal plan to stay on track.

7. Cut Sugar: Gradually reduce your sugar intake to improve overall health.

8. Whole Foods: Focus on whole, unprocessed foods in your diet.

9. Intermittent Fasting: Consider intermittent fasting for weight management and health benefits.

10. Portion Healthy Snacks: Pre-portion snacks to avoid mindless eating.

11. Diverse Diet: Incorporate a variety of fruits and vegetables into your diet.

12. Balanced Diet: Ensure your diet includes a balance of macronutrients (carbs, protein, and fat).

13. Listen to Your Body: Pay attention to hunger and fullness cues.

14. Control Emotional Eating: Find alternative ways to cope with emotions, not through food.

15. Protein at Every Meal: Include a source of protein in each meal.

16. Pre-Bedtime Snack: Have a light, protein-rich snack before bedtime for sustained energy.

17. Drink Herbal Tea: Replace sugary drinks with herbal teas.

18. Count Your Steps: Aim for 10,000 steps a day to stay active.

19. Park Farther Away: Park your car farther from your destination for extra walking.

20. Take the Stairs: Opt for stairs instead of elevators and escalators.

21. Home Workouts: Use online workout videos for home exercise.

22. Stand More: Set a reminder to stand up and move every hour.

23. Stretch Daily: Incorporate daily stretching into your routine for flexibility.

24. Quick Desk Exercises: Do desk exercises to stay active during work hours.

25. Walking Meetings: Hold meetings while walking to combine productivity and exercise.

26. Exercise Breaks: Take short exercise breaks during your workday.

27. Morning Workout Routine: Establish a consistent morning exercise routine.

28. Dance Parties: Have impromptu dance parties to get your heart rate up.

29. Hiking Adventures: Explore local trails and go hiking.

30. Stay Active with Pets: Play with your pets to stay active and bond.

31. High-Intensity Interval Training (HIIT): Incorporate HIIT workouts for efficient calorie burning.

32. Use Resistance Bands: Easily incorporate resistance band exercises at home.

33. Yoga for Flexibility: Add yoga to your routine for flexibility and relaxation.

34. Home Workstation Ergonomics: Create an ergonomic home workstation to reduce strain.

35. Regular Health Check-ups: Schedule regular check-ups and screenings.

36. Keep a Food Diary: Track your food intake to improve your diet.

37. Practice Portion Control: Use measuring cups and scales to control portions.

38. Balanced Snacking: Opt for snacks with protein and fibre for sustained energy.

39. Mindful Grocery Shopping: Stick to your grocery list and avoid impulse purchases.

40. Healthy Substitutions: Replace unhealthy ingredients with healthier alternatives.

41. Gradual Changes: Make small, gradual dietary changes for long-term success.

42. Personalized Meal Plans: Consult a nutritionist for a personalized meal plan.

43. Cooking at Home: Prepare meals at home to control ingredients and portions.

44. Hydration Reminder Apps: Use apps to remind you to drink water.

45. Spice up Your Meals: Add herbs and spices for flavour without added calories.

46. Plant-Based Days: Incorporate more plant-based meals into your dict.

47. Reduce Sodium Intake: Cut back on processed foods, which are often high in salt.

48. Read Food Labels: Pay attention to food labels and serving sizes.

49. Lean Protein Sources: Opt for lean proteins like chicken, fish, and tofu.

50. Balanced Macros: Keep an eye on your macronutrient intake.

51. Cheat Meal Day: Enjoy occasional cheat meals to stay on track long-term.

52. No Late-Night Snacking: Avoid eating late at night to improve sleep quality.

53. Breakfast Prep: Prep breakfast the night before for a quick start.

54. Healthy Smoothies: Create nutritious smoothies with fruits and veggies.

55. Balanced Meal Combinations: Pair carbohydrates with proteins and fats for balanced energy.

56. Quick Salad Dressings: Make your salad dressings to control ingredients.

57. Snack Prepping: Prepare healthy snacks to curb cravings.

58. Positive Affirmations for Health: Boost your motivation with health-focused affirmations.

59. Mindful Meal Planning: Plan your meals based on nutritional needs, not cravings.

60. Intuitive Eating: Learn to listen to your body's hunger and fullness cues.

61. Keep a Workout Journal: Track your exercise progress.

62. Try New Fitness Classes: Experiment with different fitness classes and styles.

63. Stretching Routine: Incorporate a stretching routine for flexibility.

64. Foam Rolling: Use a foam roller for post-workout recovery.

65. Invest in Workout Gear: Quality gear can enhance your exercise experience.

66. Outdoor Activities: Enjoy outdoor activities like cycling, hiking, or swimming.

67. Social Exercise: Join group fitness classes or sports teams for motivation.

68. Mindful Breathing: Practice deep breathing for relaxation and stress management.

69. Bodyweight Exercises: Use your body weight for resistance exercises.

70. Functional Fitness: Incorporate exercises that improve daily activities.

71. Customize Your Workout Playlist: Create a motivating workout playlist.

72. Virtual Personal Trainer: Use apps or videos with personal trainer guidance.

73. Mindful Rest Days: Rest days are essential for recovery; embrace them.

74. Healthy Cooking Classes: Take cooking classes to learn healthier meal preparation.

75. Savour Every Bite: Pay attention to the flavours and textures of your food.

76. Eat Slowly: Eating slowly helps prevent overeating and aids digestion.

77. Digital Detox Days: Disconnect from screens for mental and physical well-being.

78. Regular Health Screenings: Keep up with doctor appointments for early detection.

79. Cooking at Home: Preparing meals at home allows you to control ingredients.

80. Mindful Eating Habits: Pay attention to your eating habits and make necessary changes.

81. Keep a Workout Journal: Track your progress to stay motivated.

82. Social Exercise Groups: Join group classes or sports teams for social support.

83. Supportive Workout Buddy: Partner with a friend for exercise accountability.

84. Hiking Adventures: Explore local trails and enjoy the great outdoors.

85. Daily Activity Breaks: Take short breaks to stretch or walk throughout the day.

86. Virtual Health Challenges: Participate in online fitness challenges.

87. Garden for Health: Gardening is a great way to stay active and connect with nature.

88. Mindful Breathing Techniques: Practice deep breathing for relaxation.

89. Wear a Fitness Tracker: Use technology to monitor your daily activity.

90. Proper Sleep Hygiene: Prioritize sleep quality for overall well-being.

91. Mindful Meditation: Meditate to reduce stress and enhance mental clarity.

92. Learn a New Physical Skill: Challenge your body with a new skill like dancing or martial arts.

93. Varied Exercise Routine: Change up your workouts to prevent monotony.

94. Home Workouts for Convenience: Invest in home exercise equipment for convenience.

95. Morning Yoga Routine: Start the day with a calming yoga practice.

96. Active Travel: Plan trips that involve physical activity like hiking or biking.

97. Engage in Mindful Eating: Savour your meals and snacks.

98. Screen-Free Meals: Avoid screens while eating for mindful consumption.

99. Emotional Support System: Lean on friends and family for emotional support.

100. Mental Health Check-INS: Prioritize mental health with regular check-ins and self-care.

Chapter 4: Technology Hacks

Welcome to the fourth chapter of "Everyday Life Hacks: Your Guide to Navigating the Digital World." In this chapter, we'll explore 100 easy and realistic technology hacks to help you optimize your digital life, stay safe online, and make the most of the digital tools at your disposal. These hacks will empower you to enhance your productivity, security, and digital well-being.

1. Set Strong Passwords: Create complex passwords with a mix of letters, numbers, and symbols.

2. Use a Password Manager: Use a trusted password manager to generate and store passwords securely.

3. Enable Two-Factor Authentication (2FA): Add an extra layer of security to your accounts.

4. Backup Your Data: Regularly back up your important files to prevent data loss.

5. Organize Digital Files: Create a well-structured system for your digital files and folders.

6. DE clutter Your Desktop: Keep your computer desktop clean for faster access to files.

7. Regular Software Updates: Install updates for your operating system and software to patch vulnerabilities.

8. Install Reliable Antivirus Software: Protect your devices from malware and viruses.

9. Use a Virtual Private Network (VPN): Keep your online activities private and secure.

10. Clear Browser Cookies and Cache: Improve browser performance and privacy.

11. Disable Unnecessary Browser Extensions: Reduce browser clutter and potential security risks.

12. Enable Ad Blockers: Enhance web browsing speed and reduce distractions.

13. Customize Browser Start Page: Set your browser's start page to open with frequently used websites.

14. Organize Bookmarks: Create folders and tags for better bookmark management.

15. Learn Keyboard Shortcuts: Save time and navigate software and websites more efficiently.

16. Automate Repetitive Tasks: Use automation tools like IFTTT to simplify daily processes.

17. Use Cloud Storage: Access your files from anywhere with cloud storage services.

18. Customize Notifications: Limit app and email notifications to reduce distractions.

19. Archive or Delete Emails: Keep your inbox organized by archiving or deleting old emails.

20. Unsubscribe from Unwanted Emails: Reduce email clutter by unsubscribing from irrelevant lists.

21. Secure Your Wi-Fi Network: Set a strong password for your Wi-Fi to prevent unauthorized access.

22. Optimize Smartphone Settings: Adjust settings to save battery life and enhance performance.

23. Install Mobile Security Apps: Protect your smartphone from malware and phishing attacks.

24. Set up Guest Network: Keep your home Wi-Fi secure by creating a guest network.

25. Use Secure Messaging Apps: Choose end-to-end encrypted messaging apps for privacy.

26. Create Strong Mobile Device Passcodes: Protect your mobile devices with strong passcodes or biometrics.

27. Enable Device Tracking and Remote Wipe: Ensure you can locate and remotely erase lost devices.

28. Regularly Review App Permissions: Audit app permissions on your devices to protect your privacy.

29. Use a Virtual Private Network (VPN) on Mobile Devices: Secure your mobile internet connection.

30. Set Screen Time Limits: Control screen time to maintain a healthy digital balance.

31. Clear App Cache: Improve smartphone performance by clearing app cache.

32. Disable Invasive App Notifications: Disable push notifications for apps that overwhelm you.

33. Mute Group Chats: Silence noisy group chats to maintain your sanity.

34. Set Custom Ringtones and Notifications: Easily identify specific contacts or apps by sound.

35. Smartphone Task Batching: Complete similar tasks in a single smartphone session.

36. Digital Minimalism: Regularly DE clutter and reduce your digital footprint.

37. Archive or Delete Old Texts: Keep your messaging app organized by archiving or deleting old texts.

38. Use Voice Commands: Save time and multitask by using voice commands on your devices.

39. Password-Protect Sensitive Files: Secure important files with encryption or passwords.

40. Manage Social Media Time: Set limits on your daily social media use.

41. Custom Keyboard Shortcuts: Create custom keyboard shortcuts for frequently used phrases.

42. Master the Art of Copy-Paste: Use copy-paste shortcuts to save time on repetitive tasks.

43. Secure Personal Data: Lock sensitive information behind password-protected apps or files.

44. Optimize Battery Charging: Prolong your device's battery life by charging it correctly.

45. Set up a Digital Detox Routine: Dedicate tech-free time to unwind and disconnect.

46. Digital Calendar Organization: Streamline your schedule and stay on top of appointments.

47. Automate Bill Payments: Schedule automatic bill payments to avoid late fees.

48. Use Calendar Invites: Send and accept digital calendar invites for appointments and events.

49. Implement the "Two-Minute Rule": If a task can be completed in two minutes or less, do it immediately.

50. Set Smart Device Routines: Use smart speakers and devices to automate household tasks.

51. Efficient Texting: Use predictive text and swipe-typing for faster texting.

52. Effective File Search: Master the use of search features in your devices and software.

53. Manage Password Reset Information: Store security questions and password reset info securely.

54. Paperless Document Organization: Digitize and organize important documents.

55. Use Secure Messaging Apps for Work: Employ encrypted messaging apps for sensitive work communication.

56. Device Sleep Mode: Set devices to automatically enter sleep mode when not in use.

57. Emergency Contacts: Add emergency contacts to your phone for easy access in crisis situations.

58. Bookmark Organization: Categorize and tag bookmarks for efficient web browsing.

59. Customize Device Notifications: Tailor notification settings to your preferences.

60. Device Maintenance Calendar: Create a calendar to remind you to update and clean devices.

61. Limit Social Media Apps: Restrict access to social media apps to reduce time spent on them.

62. Scheduled Device Checks: Schedule regular device check-ups and updates.

63. Cloud Password Management: Store essential passwords in a secure cloud-based system.

64. Use "Do Not Disturb" Mode: Activate "Do Not Disturb" mode during focused work or relaxation.

65. Prioritize App Notifications: Choose which app notifications are most important.

66. Audio Notes for Reminders: Record audio notes for quick reminders.

67. Efficient App Arrangement: Place frequently used apps on your home screen for easy access.

68. Digital Reading Lists: Create digital lists for articles, books, and content you want to read.

69. Custom Computer Shortcuts: Create your custom keyboard shortcuts on your computer.

70. "Dark Mode" for Night Reading: Enable dark mode on apps and devices for night-time use.

71. Virtual "To-Do" Lists: Use digital to-do list apps for efficient task management.

72. Desktop Virtualization: Organize your computer desktop into virtual workspaces.

73. Use Device Tracking: Enable tracking features to locate lost or stolen devices.

74. In-App Productivity Tools: Make use of built-in productivity tools within apps and software.

75. Remote Desktop Access: Set up remote access to your home computer when away.

76. Custom App Folders: Create folders for apps based on categories or tasks.

77. Efficient Contact Management: Regularly update and organize your contacts.

78. Quick Email Sorting: Use filters and labels to automatically sort incoming emails.

79. Optimize Search Engine Usage: Learn advanced search techniques for better results.

80. Scheduled Email Time: Set specific times for checking and responding to emails.

81. Secure Social Media Accounts: Implement strong passwords and 2FA for social accounts.

82. Screen Time Monitoring: Track and analyse your screen time habits.

83. Reduce Text Notifications: Limit the number of text notifications you receive.

84. Digital Inbox Zero: Aim for a clear and organized email inbox.

85. Limit Push Notifications: Choose which apps can send you push notifications.

86. Automate Social Media Posts: Schedule social media posts in advance.

87. Clean up Digital Subscriptions: Unsubscribe from newsletters and services you no longer use.

88. Control Your Smartphone Usage: Use screen time apps to manage smartphone use.

89. Protect Your Online Privacy: Use a virtual private network (VPN) for internet browsing.

90. Digital Goal Setting: Create digital goals and track your progress.

91. Digital Task Manager: Use digital task management apps for efficient project tracking.

92. Organize Digital Photos: Sort and label digital photos for easy retrieval.

93. Secure Digital Wallets: Protect digital payment and wallet apps with strong passwords.

94. Webcam Privacy Covers: Use webcam covers for privacy when not in use.

95. Encrypt Sensitive Documents: Protect sensitive files with encryption.

96. Password-Protect Your Phone: Secure your mobile device with a strong passcode or biometrics.

97. Scheduled Device Reboots: Schedule regular device reboots to enhance performance.

98. Clear App Cache: Improve smartphone performance by clearing app cache.

99. Set Device Sleep Mode: Configure devices to enter sleep mode when not in use.

100. Update Device Firmware: Keep your devices secure with regular firmware updates.

Chapter 5: Finance Hacks

Welcome to the fifth chapter of "Everyday Life Hacks: Your Guide to Mastering Your Finances." In this chapter, we'll explore 100 easy and realistic financial hacks to help you manage your money, save, and make smarter financial decisions. These hacks will empower you to take control of your financial future and build a secure and stable financial life.

1. Create a Budget: Start by making a budget to track your income and expenses.

2. Emergency Fund: Build an emergency fund to cover unexpected expenses.

3. Set Financial Goals: Define your financial goals and make a plan to achieve them.

4. Pay Yourself First: Save a portion of your income before paying bills.

5. Automated Savings: Set up automatic transfers to your savings account.

6. Eliminate Debt: Prioritize paying off high-interest debt, such as credit cards.

7. Consolidate Debt: Consider consolidating multiple debts into a lower-interest loan.

8. Negotiate Bills: Negotiate with service providers for lower bills.

9. Check Credit Reports: Regularly review your credit reports for errors.

10. Increase Credit Score: Work on improving your credit score for better financial opportunities.

11. 24-Hour Rule: Wait 24 hours before making non-essential purchases.

12. Buy Generic Brands: Choose generic brands to save money on groceries.

13. Meal Planning: Plan meals and make grocery lists to reduce food waste.

14. Avoid Impulse Buys: Stick to your shopping list and avoid impulse purchases.

15. Shopping in Bulk: Buy non-perishable items in bulk to save on groceries.

16. Cash Envelopes: Use the envelope system for discretionary spending.

17. Negotiate Salary: Negotiate your salary during job offers and reviews.

18. Save Windfalls: Put unexpected money, like bonuses or tax refunds, into savings.

19. Student Loan Forgiveness: Research and apply for loan forgiveness programs.

20. Retirement Accounts: Maximize contributions to retirement accounts like 401(k)s.

21. Side Hustles: Consider side gigs or part-time work to boost your income.

22. House Hacking: Rent out extra space in your home to cover expenses.

23. Passive Income: Invest in sources of passive income, like dividend stocks.

24. Track Expenses: Use apps to track and categorize your expenses.

25. Refinance Loans: Explore loan refinancing options for lower interest rates.

26. Prioritize High-Interest Debt: Focus on paying off high-interest debts first.

27. Rainy Day Fund: Build a fund specifically for irregular or annual expenses.

28. Skip Extended Warranties: Avoid purchasing extended warranties on products.

29. Take Advantage of Tax Credits: Make sure you're claiming all applicable tax credits.

30. Shop Second-hand: Purchase gently used items to save on expenses.

31. Use Coupons and Discounts: Hunt for coupons and discounts before shopping.

32. Invest in Index Funds: Consider low-cost index funds for long-term investments.

33. Automate Investments: Set up automatic contributions to your investment accounts.

34. Diversify Investments: Spread investments across various asset classes.

35. Invest in Your Education: Consider courses or certifications to enhance your earning potential.

36. Use Health Savings Accounts (HSAs): Contribute to HSAs for tax-free medical expenses.

37. Refinancing Mortgages: Explore mortgage refinancing for lower rates.

38. Bundle Services: Bundle insurance and services for discounts.

39. Cancel Unused Subscriptions: Regularly review and cancel unused subscriptions.

40. Review Banking Fees: Check for hidden bank fees and switch to fee-free options.

41. Home Maintenance DIY: Learn basic home maintenance to save on repair costs.

42. Use Public Transportation: Opt for public transit to save on gas and parking.

43. Energy-Efficient Upgrades: Invest in energy-efficient appliances to lower utility bills.

44. Negotiate Rent: Discuss rent adjustments with your landlord.

45. Home Solar Panels: Explore solar panels for long-term energy savings.

46. Shop at Discount Stores: Find deals at discount and warehouse stores.

47. Set Financial Deadlines: Create deadlines for financial goals to stay accountable.

48. Use Online Calculators: Leverage online calculators to plan your financial future.

49. Retirement Catch-Up Contributions: Take advantage of catch-up contributions after age 50.

50. Cut Unused Services: Eliminate services or memberships you no longer use.

51. Avoid Lifestyle Inflation: Keep expenses in check as your income grows.

52. Grocery Shopping Timing: Shop for groceries during sales or discount periods.

53. Save Windfalls: Put unexpected money into savings or investments.

54. Health Insurance Options: Evaluate health insurance options for cost savings.

55. Buy Used Vehicles: Consider used cars to save on depreciation.

56. Review Insurance Policies: Regularly review and update insurance policies.

57. Rethink Transportation: Explore carpooling or ridesharing to cut commuting costs.

58. Pay Annual Premiums: Pay insurance premiums annually for discounts.

59. Take Advantage of Employer Benefits: Use employer benefits like gym memberships or discounts.

60. Automate Bill Payments: Schedule automatic payments to avoid late fees.

61. Limit Dining Out: Reduce dining out and opt for homemade meals.

62. Library Resources: Use the library for books, movies, and digital resources.

63. Review Investment Fees: Ensure investment fees aren't eating into your returns.

64. Financial Independence, Retire Early (FIRE): Explore the FIRE movement for early retirement planning.

65. Reuse and Recycle: Up cycle or recycle items instead of buying new.

66. Kids' College Savings: Start a college fund for your child's education.

67. Plan Frugal Vacations: Enjoy budget-friendly vacations.

68. Buy Quality, Not Quantity: Invest in quality items that last longer.

69. DIY Home Repairs: Tackle simple home repairs yourself to save on labour costs.

70. Homemade Gifts: Create personalized gifts instead of buying expensive ones.

71. Revaluate Streaming Services: Downsize streaming subscriptions to essential ones.

72. Sell Unwanted Items: DE clutter and make money by selling unused items.

73. Save Spare Change: Collect spare change in a jar or digital savings app.

74. Energy-Saving Light Bulbs: Use energy-efficient light bulbs to lower electricity costs.

75. No-Spend Challenges: Dedicate periods to restrict unnecessary spending.

76. Barter or Trade Services: Exchange services or goods with others.

77. Price Comparison Tools: Use price comparison websites and apps when shopping.

78. Meal Prepping: Prepare meals in advance to reduce restaurant spending.

79. Limit ATM Fees: Use your bank's ATMs to avoid fees.

80. Open a High-Yield Savings Account: Earn more interest on your savings.

81. Negotiate Home Repairs: Get multiple quotes and negotiate for home repairs.

82. Auto Maintenance DIY: Learn basic car maintenance to reduce repair costs.

83. Save Windfalls for Retirement: Put unexpected money into your retirement account.

84. Pay Bills on Time: Avoid late fees by paying bills promptly.

85. Delayed Gratification: Train yourself to save and wait for bigger purchases.

86. Avoid Gambling and Lottery Tickets: Stay away from gambling for a better financial future.

87. Freelancing and Gig Economy Work: Use your skills for freelance or gig work.

88. Trade Your Skills: Exchange services with others, like tutoring for gardening help.

89. Energy-Efficient Home Upgrades: Invest in energy-efficient home improvements.

90. Yard Sales and Thrifting: Find bargains at yard sales and thrift stores.

91. Insurance Deductibles: Opt for higher insurance deductibles to lower premiums.

92. Cancel Unused Gym Memberships: Stop paying for underused gym memberships.

93. 30-Day Rule for Purchases: Wait 30 days before buying non-essential items.

94. Refurbished Electronics: Consider refurbished tech products for savings.

95. Utilize Rewards Programs: Make use of loyalty and rewards programs.

96. Pet Health Savings: Set aside funds for pet emergencies and health costs.

97. Financial Review: Regularly review your financial situation and make adjustments.

98. Cut Unnecessary Subscriptions: Cancel underused subscriptions and services.

99. Reduce Entertainment Spending: Explore low-cost or free entertainment options.

100. Share Expenses: Split costs with friends or family for shared activities.

Chapter 6: Travel Hacks

Welcome to the sixth chapter of "Everyday Life Hacks: Your Guide to Stress-Free Travel." In this chapter, we'll explore 100 easy and realistic travel hacks to help you plan, enjoy, and make the most of your journeys. These hacks cover everything from trip preparation and packing to in-flight comfort and exploring new destinations, ensuring your travels are smooth and memorable.

1. Plan Your Itinerary: Research and outline your travel plans before you go.

2. Travel Off-Peak: Choose off-peak travel times for lower costs and fewer crowds.

3. Use Fare Comparison Sites: Compare airfares on multiple websites for the best deals.

4. Join Frequent Flyer Programs: Earn miles and perks by signing up for frequent flyer programs.

5. Travel Insurance: Invest in travel insurance for peace of mind.

6. Packing List: Create a comprehensive packing list to avoid forgetting essentials.

7. Roll Clothes: Roll clothes instead of folding for more efficient packing.

8. Use Packing Cubes: Organize and compress clothing with packing cubes.

9. Limit Shoes: Pack versatile shoes to save space in your luggage.

10. Travel-Size Toiletries: Use travel-size toiletries to reduce bulk.

11. Photocopies of Important Documents: Make copies of passports, tickets, and travel insurance.

12. Share Your Itinerary: Share your travel itinerary with a trusted person back home.

13. Prepare a Digital Itinerary: Keep digital copies of travel plans on your smartphone.

14. Scan Important Documents: Scan important documents and save them in cloud storage.

15. Bring a Reusable Water Bottle: Stay hydrated on your journey without buying bottled water.

16. Noise-Cancelling Headphones: Block out noise during your flight with noise-cancelling headphones.

17. Carry an Extra Power Bank: Always have a power bank for your devices.

18. In-Flight Entertainment: Download movies and shows for offline viewing.

19. Compression Socks: Wear compression socks to reduce swelling on long flights.

20. Dress in Layers: Dress in layers for comfort in fluctuating cabin temperatures.

21. Seat Selection: Choose the best seat based on your needs and preferences.

22. Sanitize Your Space: Wipe down your seat and tray table with sanitizing wipes.

23. Stay Hydrated: Drink water throughout your flight to avoid dehydration.

24. Adapt to Local Time: Adjust to the local time zone as soon as you arrive.

25. Local Currency: Carry local currency for small purchases.

26. Map Apps: Download offline maps for easy navigation.

27. Learn Basic Phrases: Learn a few local phrases for courtesy and communication.

28. Avoid Crowded Attractions: Visit popular attractions early in the day or late in the evening.

29. Skip Lines: Consider purchasing skip-the-line tickets for popular sites.

30. Group Tours: Join group tours for convenience and local insights.

31. Check Visa Requirements: Confirm visa requirements for your destination.

32. Local SIM Card: Buy a local SIM card for affordable data and calls.

33. Travel Wallet: Use a secure, RFID-blocking travel wallet.

34. Personal Safety Alarms: Carry personal safety alarms for added security.

35. Offline Translation Apps: Download offline translation apps for language support.

36. Use Public Transportation: Save money by using public transportation.

37. City Passes: Explore city passes for discounts on multiple attractions.

38. Eat Where Locals Eat: Savour authentic cuisine by dining where locals go.

39. Pack Snacks: Carry snacks for on-the-go energy.

40. Learn Local Etiquette: Familiarize yourself with local customs to show respect.

41. Travel-Size Laundry Detergent: Wash clothes in the sink with travel-size detergent.

42. Universal Power Adapter: Bring a universal power adapter for your devices.

43. Electronic Boarding Pass: Use digital boarding passes to save paper.

44. Carry Extra Ziploc Bags: Use them for organizing and keeping items dry.

45. Stash Emergency Cash: Hide emergency cash in a discreet place.

46. Learn the 3-1-1 Rule: Follow TSA's 3-1-1 rule for carrying liquids.

47. In-Flight Hydration: Use a hydrating facial spray to combat dry cabin air.

48. Lightweight Luggage: Choose lightweight luggage to maximize packing capacity.

49. Travel-Sized Laundry Line: Hang clothes with a portable laundry line.

50. Disguised Valuables Pouch: Use a hidden pouch for valuable items.

51. Pre-download Maps: Download maps for your destination for offline use.

52. RFID-Blocking Passport Holder: Protect your passport from unauthorized scanning.

53. Consider Travel Insurance: Evaluate your destination's safety and consider travel insurance.

54. Flexible Dates: Be flexible with travel dates for better deals.

55. Priority Pass: Join a lounge access program for airport relaxation.

56. Lounge Buddy App: Find and access airport lounges with the Lounge Buddy app.

57. Join a Loyalty Program: Enrol in loyalty programs for hotels and airlines.

58. Research Airport Transportation: Find the most cost-effective way to reach your accommodations.

59. In-Flight Amenities: Explore in-flight amenities and choose your airline accordingly.

60. Know Baggage Policies: Understand baggage policies and fees before packing.

61. Airport Security Preparation: Prepare for security checks to expedite the process.

62. Extra Ziploc Bags: Pack extra Ziploc bags for various uses.

63. TSA PreCheck or Global Entry: Consider expedited security programs for frequent travellers.

64. Backup Travel Documents: Store digital copies of travel documents in a secure cloud service.

65. In-Flight Exercises: Stretch and move on long flights to prevent stiffness.

66. Budget Ahead: Plan your daily expenses to stick to your travel budget.

67. Review Your Medical Coverage: Check if your health insurance covers international travel.

68. Accommodation Reviews: Read online reviews to find reliable accommodations.

69. Google Maps Offline: Download offline maps for navigation without internet.

70. Stay Charged: Bring portable chargers for your devices.

71. Travel Journal: Keep a travel journal for memories and reflections.

72. Secure Your Backpack: Lock your backpack's zippers when in crowded areas.

73. Backup Bank and Credit Cards: Bring a spare debit and credit card in case one is lost.

74. Copy Important Documents: Leave copies of your passport and other documents with a trusted contact.

75. GPS Tracker for Luggage: Use a GPS tracker to locate lost luggage.

76. Public Restrooms: Carry tissues and hand sanitizer for public restrooms.

77. Use a Money Belt: Wear a money belt to secure your valuables.

78. Local SIM Card Apps: Download local apps for transportation and communication.

79. Travel-Friendly Apps: Use travel apps for navigation and local tips.

80. Buy Travel Insurance: Consider travel insurance for unexpected cancellations or delays.

81. Solo Travel Safety: Let someone know your daily plans when traveling solo.

82. Medication Backup: Carry extra medications in case of travel delays.

83. Currency Conversion App: Download a currency conversion app for real-time rates.

84. Respect Local Traditions: Learn about and respect local customs.

85. Online Ticket Booking: Purchase tickets for attractions online to avoid lines.

86. Research Local Scams: Be aware of common scams at your destination.

87. Dual Voltage Electronics: Bring dual-voltage electronic devices for international travel.

88. Keep Travel-Size Toiletries: Collect travel-size toiletries from hotels.

89. Use Public Restrooms: Take advantage of clean, free public restrooms.

90. Hotel Shuttle Services: Use free hotel shuttle services when available.

91. Take Walking Tours: Join free walking tours for local insights.

92. Stay with Locals: Explore homestays or vacation rentals for local experiences.

93. Use Hotel Safes: Store valuables in hotel room safes.

94. Know Exchange Rates: Understand the local currency exchange rate.

95. Get Vaccinations: Stay up-to-date on recommended vaccinations for your destination.

96. Share an Itinerary: Share your travel itinerary with friends or family.

97. Email Yourself: Email travel documents to yourself for easy access.

98. Carry a Portable Door Lock: Enhance security in your accommodations with a portable door lock.

99. Learn Basic Language Phrases: Familiarize yourself with a few key phrases in the local language.

100. Travel Pillow and Blanket: Carry a travel pillow and small blanket for added comfort.

Chapter 7: Home Improvement Hacks

Welcome to the seventh chapter of "Everyday Life Hacks: Your Guide to Transforming Your Living Space." In this chapter, we'll explore 100 easy and realistic home improvement hacks to help you enhance your living space, from maximizing organization and efficiency to beautifying your home and maintaining its value. These hacks will empower you to make the most of your space and create a comfortable and welcoming home.

1. DE clutter Regularly: Make DE cluttering a regular habit to keep your home tidy.

2. Prioritize Safety: Ensure your home is safe with working smoke detectors and carbon monoxide alarms.

3. Create a Home Maintenance Schedule: Plan and schedule regular home maintenance tasks.

4. DIY Repair Skills: Learn basic DIY repair skills to handle minor issues.

5. Efficient Cleaning Supplies: Invest in quality cleaning supplies for effective cleaning.

6. Deep Clean the Refrigerator: Remove and clean refrigerator shelves and drawers.

7. Freshen up the Garbage Disposal: Use citrus peels or baking soda to deodorize the garbage disposal.

8. Microwave Cleaning Trick: Place a microwave-safe bowl with water and lemon slices inside, then heat for a few minutes for easy cleaning.

9. DIY Air Fresheners: Make homemade air fresheners with essential oils and water.

10. Remove Carpet Stains: Use a mixture of vinegar and water to remove carpet stains.

11. Prevent Grout Mould: Apply a mixture of baking soda and water to grout to prevent mould.

12. Dryer Vent Cleaning: Clean the dryer vent to prevent lint build-up and improve efficiency.

13. Maintain the HVAC System: Change HVAC filters regularly and have your system serviced.

14. Garage Organization: Create an organized space in your garage for storage.

15. Bathroom Ventilation: Use the bathroom fan or open a window during and after showers to prevent mould.

16. Install a Programmable Thermostat: Save energy by programming your thermostat.

17. Repair Leaky Faucets: Fix leaky faucets to save water and money.

18. Reuse Old Furniture: Repurpose old furniture to give it new life.

19. Maintain the Lawn: Regularly mow and maintain your lawn for curb appeal.

20. Weather-strip Doors and Windows: Use weather-stripping to prevent drafts.

21. Energy-Efficient Light Bulbs: Replace incandescent bulbs with energy-efficient LED or CFL bulbs.

22. Ceiling Fan Rotation: Adjust ceiling fan rotation for seasonal comfort.

23. Proper Garbage Disposal Use: Dispose of food waste properly to avoid clogs.

24. Prevent Pest Infestations: Seal cracks and gaps to prevent pests from entering your home.

25. Organize Kitchen Cabinets: Use shelf organizers and dividers to maximize cabinet space.

26. Deep-Clean the Oven: Remove oven racks and clean the oven thoroughly.

27. Effective Dishwasher Cleaning: Clean the dishwasher with vinegar and baking soda to remove residue.

28. Manage Junk Mail: Reduce junk mail by unsubscribing from mailing lists.

29. Energy-Efficient Appliances: Invest in energy-efficient appliances for long-term savings.

30. Fix Squeaky Floors: Repair squeaky floors with a squeak-reducing kit.

31. Upgrade Insulation: Improve insulation for better temperature control.

32. Maintain Gutters: Clean gutters regularly to prevent clogs and water damage.

33. Wallpaper Revamp: Use removable wallpaper for a quick room transformation.

34. Garden Bed Maintenance: Keep garden beds weed-free and well-maintained.

35. DIY Paint Touch-Ups: Keep extra paint for quick touch-ups on walls and furniture.

36. Repurpose Jars: Reuse glass jars for storage or decorative purposes.

37. Energy-Efficient Windows: Upgrade to energy-efficient windows for better insulation.

38. Reorganize the Closet: DE clutter and organize your closet to save time.

39. Create a Family Command Centre: Establish a central hub for family schedules and communication.

40. Regularly Clean Air Ducts: Maintain clean air ducts for better indoor air quality.

41. Green Cleaning Products: Use eco-friendly cleaning products to reduce chemical exposure.

42. Get Rid of Old Electronics: Recycle or dispose of old electronics properly.

43. Wall-Mounted Shelves: Install wall-mounted shelves for additional storage.

44. Childproofing: Childproof your home for safety.

45. DIY Pest Control: Use natural remedies to control common pests.

46. Efficient Fridge Organization: Keep frequently used items at eye level in the fridge.

47. Home Office Organization: Organize your home office for productivity.

48. Water Heater Maintenance: Flush your water heater to remove sediment.

49. Redo Caulk and Grout: Replace caulk and grout in bathrooms and kitchens.

50. Emergency Preparedness Kit: Create an emergency kit with essential supplies.

51. Closet Under-Bed Storage: Utilize storage containers under the bed.

52. Create a Seasonal Checklist: Make a list of seasonal home maintenance tasks.

53. Organize Kitchen Drawers: Use dividers to organize kitchen utensil drawers.

54. Outdoor Entertainment Area: Create an inviting outdoor space for relaxation.

55. Creative Wall Art: Use removable wall decals or art to add character to your home.

56. Maximize Vertical Space: Install hooks and shelves on walls for extra storage.

57. Eco-Friendly Landscaping: Choose low-maintenance, drought-tolerant plants for landscaping.

58. Indoor Plant Care: Learn to care for indoor plants for better air quality and aesthetics.

59. Reupholster Furniture: Give old furniture a new look with reupholstering.

60. DIY Shelving Units: Build your own shelving units for a custom look.

61. Efficient Laundry Room Design: Optimize your laundry room for efficiency.

62. Up cycled Decor: Repurpose old items into home decor.

63. Bathroom Space Savers: Use over-the-toilet storage for additional bathroom space.

64. Garden Irrigation System: Install an irrigation system for efficient watering.

65. DIY Closet Renovation: Redesign your closet for better organization.

66. Home Automation: Incorporate smart home devices for convenience.

67. Upgrade Kitchen Appliances: Invest in energy-efficient and high-quality kitchen appliances.

68. Sealing Drafts: Seal gaps and drafts around windows and doors.

69. Install Crown Moulding: Add crown moulding for a touch of elegance.

70. DIY Storage Solutions: Create custom storage solutions for your home.

71. Energy-Efficient Water Heater: Upgrade to an energy-efficient water heater.

72. Install a Home Security System: Improve home security with a modern system.

73. Insulate Attic and Basement: Insulate these areas for better temperature control.

74. Replace Cabinet Hardware: Update your kitchen or bathroom by changing cabinet hardware.

75. Energy-Efficient Showerheads: Install low-flow showerheads to save water.

76. Upgrade Light Fixtures: Replace outdated light fixtures for a fresh look.

77. Fresh Paint: Use a fresh coat of paint to transform a room.

78. DIY Backsplash: Create a custom backsplash for your kitchen.

79. Window Treatments: Use curtains and blinds for privacy and insulation.

80. Garden Lighting: Install outdoor lighting for safety and aesthetics.

81. Chalkboard Wall: Paint a wall with chalkboard paint for messages and art.

82. Organize the Garage: Turn your garage into an organized workspace.

83. Install a Bathroom Ventilation Fan: Prevent moisture build-up in the bathroom.

84. Green Home Improvements: Consider energy-efficient and eco-friendly upgrades.

85. Paint Your Front Door: Give your home curb appeal with a fresh front door colour.

86. Expand Your Storage: Use under-stair storage for more room.

87. Energy-Efficient Thermostat: Install a programmable thermostat for temperature control.

88. Energy-Efficient Appliances: Upgrade to appliances with the Energy Star label.

89. Small Bathroom Storage: Use wall-mounted storage in small bathrooms.

90. DIY Artwork: Create your own artwork for personalized decor.

91. Maximize Garage Space: Install wall-mounted storage in the garage.

92. Attic Conversion: Convert your attic into a functional space.

93. Re-Caulk the Bathtub: Renew the seal around your bathtub for a fresh look.

94. Dress up Your Front Yard: Add landscaping and garden decor for curb appeal.

95. Built-In Bookshelves: Build bookshelves into empty wall spaces.

96. Redo Kitchen Countertops: Give your kitchen a new look with updated countertops.

97. Revive Your Deck: Restore and refinish your deck for outdoor enjoyment.

98. Backyard Patio: Create a comfortable outdoor living area on your patio.

99. Wallpaper Accent Wall: Use wallpaper on an accent wall for a unique touch.

100. Home Office Renovation: Redesign your home office for productivity and comfort.

Chapter 8: Cooking and Food Hacks

Welcome to the eighth chapter of "Everyday Life Hacks: Your Guide to Mastering the Kitchen." In this chapter, we'll explore 100 easy and realistic cooking and food hacks to help you become a more efficient, creative, and confident cook. These hacks will cover everything from meal planning and grocery shopping to food storage and kitchen organization, ensuring that your time in the kitchen is both enjoyable and productive.

1. Meal Planning: Plan your meals for the week to save time and reduce food waste.

2. Grocery List: Create a shopping list based on your meal plan to avoid impulse buying.

3. Shop Seasonal: Buy fruits and vegetables when they're in season for the best flavour and price.

4. Batch Cooking: Prepare large batches of food and freeze them in individual portions.

5. Knife Skills: Learn basic knife skills to cut and chop more efficiently.

6. Store Fresh Herbs: Keep fresh herbs in a glass of water in the refrigerator.

7. Minimize Food Waste: Use leftover vegetables in a stir-fry or omelette.

8. Boiling Water Faster: Cover pots with lids to boil water more quickly.

9. Easy Peel Boiled Eggs: Add a teaspoon of baking soda to the water for easy-to-peel boiled eggs.

10. Keep Brown Sugar Soft: Place a slice of bread or a damp paper towel in the sugar container.

11. Soften Butter Quickly: Grate cold butter to soften it faster.

12. Make Homemade Croutons: Use stale bread to make homemade croutons.

13. Quick Garlic Peeling: Place garlic cloves in a jar and shake vigorously to peel.

14. Easy Pancake Mix: Store pancake batter in a squeeze bottle for mess-free pancakes.

15. Grate Frozen Butter: Use a cheese grater to add cold butter to recipes.

16. DIY Buttermilk: Add one tablespoon of vinegar or lemon juice to a cup of milk for buttermilk.

17. Prevent over boiling: Place a wooden spoon across a pot to prevent it from boiling over.

18. Efficient Lemon Squeezer: Use kitchen tongs to squeeze citrus fruits.

19. Instant Iced Coffee: Pour hot coffee over ice cubes for an instant iced coffee.

20. Ripen Avocados Quickly: Place avocados in a paper bag with a banana to speed up ripening.

21. Fresh Coffee Beans: Grind coffee beans just before brewing for the best flavour.

22. Natural Non-Stick Cooking: Season cast-iron pans with oil to create a non-stick surface.

23. Revive Stale Bread: Sprinkle stale bread with water and reheat in the oven.

24. Separating Egg Yolks: Use an empty plastic bottle to separate egg yolks from whites.

25. Extend the Life of Bananas: Wrap the stem of a bunch of bananas with plastic wrap to extend their freshness.

26. Cheese Grating Trick: Freeze cheese for easier grating.

27. No-Tear Onion Chopping: Chill onions in the freezer before chopping to reduce tears.

28. Perfectly Poached Eggs: Use a muffin tin to make multiple poached eggs at once.

29. Soften Brown Sugar: Place a piece of apple in a container with hardened brown sugar.

30. Freezer Bag Hack: Use a clothespin to keep a freezer bag upright while filling it.

31. Make Perfect Rice: Rinse rice before cooking to remove excess starch.

32. Reheat Pizza Perfectly: Reheat pizza slices in a skillet for a crispy crust.

33. Check Egg Freshness: Place an egg in a bowl of water; if it sinks, it's fresh; if it floats, it's not.

34. Juice Citrus Fruit Easily: Roll a lemon or lime on the counter before juicing.

35. Open Jars with Rubber Gloves: Use rubber gloves to improve your grip when opening stubborn jars.

36. Prevent Foaming Pasta Water: Place a wooden spoon across a pot to prevent pasta water from foaming over.

37. Fresh Salad Greens: Store washed lettuce or spinach with a paper towel to absorb moisture.

38. Easy Ice Cream Scooping: Run your ice cream scooper under hot water to make scooping easier.

39. Creative Leftovers: Turn leftovers into new dishes, like using last night's chicken in a sandwich.

40. Homemade Crispy Fries: Coat potato wedges in corn-starch before baking for extra crispiness.

41. Quick Marinade: Use a fork to pierce meat before marinating to allow flavours to penetrate.

42. Perfectly Cooked Meat: Use a meat thermometer to ensure meat is cooked to the right temperature.

43. Easier Apple Slicing: Use an apple slicer to quickly cut apples into uniform pieces.

44. Homemade Smoothies: Freeze overripe fruit for future smoothies.

45. Keep Freshness in Bread: Store bread with a celery stick to keep it fresh longer.

46. Melt Chocolate Perfectly: Melt chocolate in a microwave with short, 15-second bursts.

47. Homemade Whipped Cream: Use a chilled bowl and beaters to make homemade whipped cream.

48. Efficient Banana Peeling: Peel a banana from the bottom for less stringy bits.

49. Extend Tomato Freshness: Store tomatoes at room temperature to retain flavour.

50. Keep Baking Supplies Fresh: Keep baking soda and powder in airtight containers to prevent clumping.

51. Perfectly Cooked Pasta: Toss pasta with sauce in a pan for even coating.

52. Easy Citrus Zesting: Use a micro plane grater to zest citrus fruits.

53. Flavourful Broths: Save vegetable scraps and meat bones for homemade broths.

54. Make Your Own Sauces: Create custom sauces using ketchup and various spices.

55. Cooking Wine Ice Cubes: Freeze leftover cooking wine in ice cube trays for future use.

56. Homemade Flavoured Butter: Mix herbs and spices into softened butter for a custom spread.

57. Cook Perfect Rice: Use a kitchen towel under the pot lid to prevent steam from escaping.

58. Ripen Tomatoes Quickly: Place unripe tomatoes in a paper bag to speed up ripening.

59. Double Duty Citrus: Use the juice and zest of lemons and limes for added flavour.

60. Easy Gravy Fat Separation: Use a gravy separator to remove fat from sauces.

61. Salad Dressing Mixer: Use a mason jar for easy salad dressing mixing.

62. Muffin Tin Meatloaf: Use a muffin tin to make mini meatloaves for easy portioning.

63. Rice Krispies Treats Coating: Grease your hands with butter when making Rice Krispies treats to prevent sticking.

64. DIY Whipped Topping: Whip canned coconut milk for a dairy-free whipped topping.

65. Quick Avocado Peeling: Slice and scoop out ripe avocados for easy peeling.

66. Efficient Bacon Cooking: Bake bacon in the oven for even cooking and less mess.

67. Food Processor Efficiency: Use a food processor to quickly chop vegetables.

68. Perfect Pancake Pouring: Use a squeeze bottle for precise pancake pouring.

69. Food Storage Organization: Label and date containers in the freezer for easy identification.

70. Freeze Fresh Herbs: Freeze fresh herbs in oil for convenient use in recipes.

71. Prevent Sticky Rice: Rinse rice well before cooking to reduce stickiness.

72. Prevent Pot Boil-Overs: Place a wooden spoon over a boiling pot to prevent spills.

73. Revive Stale Bread: Refresh stale bread by wrapping it in a damp towel and reheating it in the oven.

74. Preserve Freshness: Keep mushrooms in a paper bag to maintain their texture.

75. No-Mess Taco Filling: Use a stand-up taco shell holder for mess-free filling.

76. Soften Brown Sugar: Add an apple slice to a container of hardened brown sugar.

77. Easy Onion Dicing: Score an onion before chopping for even and efficient dicing.

78. Check Egg Freshness: Test eggs by placing them in water; fresh eggs sink, bad ones float.

79. Peel Ginger with a Spoon: Use a spoon to easily peel ginger without waste.

80. Perfectly Poached Eggs: Use a mesh strainer to achieve beautifully poached eggs.

81. Frozen Herb Cubes: Freeze fresh herbs in ice cube trays with water for easy use in cooking.

82. No-Mess Pomegranate Seeding: Open a pomegranate underwater to avoid staining.

83. Fresh Coffee Beans: Grind coffee beans just before brewing for the best flavour.

84. Fast Avocado Slicing: Score an avocado in the shell before scooping out the flesh.

85. Thaw Meat Safely: Thaw meat in the refrigerator or in a sealed plastic bag under cold water.

86. Fluffy Omelettes: Add a pinch of corn-starch to omelettes for extra fluffiness.

87. Soften Butter Quickly: Grate cold butter to soften it faster.

88. Homemade Butter Spreader: Use dental floss to slice cold butter for spreading.

89. Easy Tomato Peeling: Boil tomatoes briefly, then transfer them to ice water for easy peeling.

90. Juicy Burgers: Add a small ice cube in the centre of your burger patty to keep it juicy.

91. Make Your Own Breadcrumbs: Use a food processor to turn stale bread into breadcrumbs.

92. Citrus Juice Freshness: Microwave citrus fruits for 10-15 seconds to make juicing easier.

93. Sift Flour without a Sifter: Use a fine-mesh strainer to sift flour.

94. Speedy Garlic Peeling: Shake garlic cloves vigorously inside two bowls to remove the peel.

95. Efficient Pancake Flip: Flip pancakes with a quick and confident wrist motion.

96. Juicy Meatloaf: Add shredded zucchini to meatloaf for extra moisture.

97. Soften Ice Cream Easily: Microwave an ice cream scoop for easy serving.

98. Perfectly Toasted Nuts: Toast nuts in a dry skillet for a rich, nutty flavour.

99. Melt Chocolate in a Bowl: Place a heatproof bowl over simmering water for controlled chocolate melting.

100. Homemade Crispy Fries: Soak potato wedges in cold water before baking for extra crispiness.

Chapter 9: Cleaning Hacks

Welcome to the ninth chapter of "Everyday Life Hacks: Your Guide to a Spotless Home." In this chapter, we'll explore 100 easy and realistic cleaning hacks to help you maintain a clean and organized living space. These hacks will cover various aspects of cleaning, from tackling tough stains and cleaning efficiently to maintaining a tidy and fresh home. With these hacks, you'll save time and energy while achieving a cleaner and more inviting environment.

1. Create a Cleaning Schedule: Establish a cleaning routine to stay on top of tasks.

2. Organize Cleaning Supplies: Keep cleaning supplies in one place for easy access.

3. DIY All-Purpose Cleaner: Create an eco-friendly all-purpose cleaner with vinegar and water.

4. Baking Soda Deodorizer: Use baking soda to eliminate odours from carpets and upholstery.

5. Lemon for Microwave Cleaning: Heat a lemon in the microwave to soften grime for easy cleaning.

6. Remove Hard Water Stains: Use vinegar and a scrubbing sponge to remove hard water stains.

7. Tackle Oven Grease: Sprinkle baking soda, then spray with vinegar, and scrub oven grease away.

8. Freshen Mattress with Baking Soda: Sprinkle baking soda on your mattress, let it sit, then vacuum.

9. De-Gunk a Toaster: Clean toaster crumbs with a pastry brush.

10. Stainless Steel Shine: Polish stainless steel appliances with olive oil for a brilliant shine.

11. Dust Electronics with Coffee Filters: Use coffee filters to dust screens and electronics.

12. Clean Grout with Toothpaste: Apply toothpaste and scrub grout for a brighter look.

13. Microfiber Magic: Use microfiber cloths to clean surfaces without streaks.

14. Blinds Cleaning Hack: Wrap a microfiber cloth around tongs for efficient blind cleaning.

15. Carpet Stain Removal: Blot stains with a mixture of vinegar and water, then sprinkle with baking soda.

16. Freshen up Dishwasher: Place a cup of vinegar in an empty dishwasher and run a cycle.

17. Vacuum Trick for Pet Hair: Use a squeegee on carpets to remove pet hair.

18. Natural Wood Polish: Combine olive oil and lemon juice for natural wood polish.

19. Brighten Toilet Bowl: Drop a denture cleaning tablet into the toilet bowl for a quick clean.

20. Clean Shower Head with Vinegar: Fill a bag with vinegar and secure it around the showerhead to remove build-up.

21. Banish Baseboard Dust: Attach a dryer sheet to a paint roller for easy baseboard dusting.

22. Grime-Free Blender: Blend soapy water for a quick blender cleaning.

23. Freshen Garbage Disposal: Toss citrus peels and ice cubes into the disposal for a fresh scent.

24. Sparkling Window Tracks: Use a toothbrush and vinegar to scrub window tracks.

25. DIY Gunk Remover: Mix baking soda and coconut oil to remove sticky residues.

26. Remove Carpet Indentations: Place ice cubes on carpet indentations, then fluff with a fork.

27. Speedy Sponge Sanitization: Microwave a wet sponge for a minute to kill bacteria.

28. Vacuum Ceiling Fan Blades: Use a pillowcase to capture dust while cleaning fan blades.

29. Clean Oven Racks in a Bag: Place oven racks in a garbage bag with ammonia for easy cleaning.

30. Squeegee Pet Hair from Carpets: Run a squeegee across carpets to gather pet hair.

31. Stainless Steel Appliance Fingerprints: Wipe away fingerprints with a cloth and a bit of baby oil.

32. Lint Roller Lampshades: Use a lint roller to clean lampshades.

33. Wipe Down Light Switches: Regularly clean light switches with a disinfectant wipe.

34. Deep Clean Cutting Boards with Salt: Scrub cutting boards with salt and a lemon half.

35. Remove Stickers with Hairdryer: Warm stickers with a hairdryer to ease removal.

36. Oven Mitt Dusting: Use an oven mitt to dust surfaces.

37. Remove Carpet Stains with Iron: Place a cloth soaked in vinegar over carpet stains and iron to remove.

38. Speedy Trash Can Cleaning: Rinse out trash cans with a hose for a quick clean.

39. No-Scrub Bathtub Cleaning: Combine equal parts of vinegar and dish soap in a scrubbing wand for no-scrub bathtub cleaning.

40. DIY Disinfecting Wipes: Make your disinfecting wipes with paper towels and a cleaning solution.

41. Freshen Garbage Cans: Place a coffee filter at the bottom of your garbage can to absorb odours.

42. Instant Blind Cleaning: Use a sock over your hand to quickly clean blinds.

43. Natural Toilet Bowl Cleaner: Sprinkle baking soda, then add vinegar for an eco-friendly toilet bowl cleaner.

44. Shiny Chrome Faucets: Rub chrome faucets with baby oil for extra shine.

45. Remove Grease Stains with Chalk: Rub chalk on clothing to absorb and lift grease stains.

46. Sparkling Shower Doors: Clean shower doors with a mixture of vinegar and dish soap.

47. DIY Sink Cleaner: Combine baking soda and water to make a sink-cleaning paste.

48. Fabric Softener Dusting: Use a fabric softener sheet to dust surfaces.

49. Speedy Blind Cleaning with Tongs: Wrap microfiber cloths around tongs for efficient blind cleaning.

50. Clean Blender with Soapy Water: Blend soapy water for a quick blender clean.

51. No-Scrub Microwave: Fill a bowl with water and vinegar, microwave it, and easily wipe away grime.

52. Remove Coffee Stains with Salt: Mix salt and dish soap to remove coffee stains from mugs.

53. Disinfect Sponges in the Microwave: Microwave damp sponges for a minute to disinfect them.

54. Clean and Deodorize Garbage Disposal: Use lemon slices and ice cubes to clean and deodorize the disposal.

55. Grout cleaning with a Toothbrush: Use an old toothbrush and a baking soda paste to clean grout.

56. Refresh Refrigerator with Vanilla Extract: Soak a cotton ball in vanilla extract and place it in the fridge for a fresh scent.

57. Remove Rust with Salt and Lime: Scrub rust with salt and a lime for effective rust removal.

58. Lint Roller Lampshades: Use a lint roller to quickly clean lampshades.

59. Sparkling Jewellery with Toothpaste: Gently scrub jewellery with toothpaste for added shine.

60. Wipe Down Light Switches: Regularly clean light switches with a disinfectant wipe.

61. Microwave Cleaning with Lemon: Microwave a bowl of water with lemon slices to loosen grime.

62. DIY Gunk Remover: Mix baking soda and coconut oil to remove sticky residues.

63. Oven Mitt Dusting: Use an oven mitt to dust surfaces.

64. Lint Roller Dusting: Use a lint roller for quick and effective dusting.

65. Remove Carpet Indentations: Place ice cubes on carpet indentations, then fluff with a fork.

66. Vacuum Ceiling Fan Blades: Use a pillowcase to capture dust while cleaning fan blades.

67. Deep Clean Cutting Boards with Salt: Scrub cutting boards with salt and a lemon half.

68. Remove Stickers with Hairdryer: Warm stickers with a hairdryer to ease removal.

69. DIY Disinfecting Wipes: Make your disinfecting wipes with paper towels and a cleaning solution.

70. Freshen Garbage Cans: Place a coffee filter at the bottom of your garbage can to absorb odours.

71. Instant Blind Cleaning: Use a sock over your hand to quickly clean blinds.

72. No-Scrub Bathtub Cleaning: Combine equal parts of vinegar and dish soap in a scrubbing wand for no-scrub bathtub cleaning.

73. Natural Toilet Bowl Cleaner: Sprinkle baking soda, then add vinegar for an eco-friendly toilet bowl cleaner.

74. Shiny Chrome Faucets: Rub chrome faucets with baby oil for extra shine.

75. Remove Grease Stains with Chalk: Rub chalk on clothing to absorb and lift grease stains.

76. Sparkling Shower Doors: Clean shower doors with a mixture of vinegar and dish soap.

77. DIY Sink Cleaner: Combine baking soda and water to make a sink-cleaning paste.

78. Fabric Softener Dusting: Use a fabric softener sheet to dust surfaces.

79. Speedy Blind Cleaning with Tongs: Wrap microfiber cloths around tongs for efficient blind cleaning.

80. Clean Blender with Soapy Water: Blend soapy water for a quick blender clean.

81. No-Scrub Microwave: Fill a bowl with water and vinegar, microwave it, and easily wipe away grime.

82. Remove Coffee Stains with Salt: Mix salt and dish soap to remove coffee stains from mugs.

83. Disinfect Sponges in the Microwave: Microwave damp sponges for a minute to disinfect them.

84. Clean and Deodorize Garbage Disposal: Use lemon slices and ice cubes to clean and deodorize the disposal.

85. Grout cleaning with a Toothbrush: Use an old toothbrush and a baking soda paste to clean grout.

86. Refresh Refrigerator with Vanilla Extract: Soak a cotton ball in vanilla extract and place it in the fridge for a fresh scent.

87. Remove Rust with Salt and Lime: Scrub rust with salt and a lime for effective rust removal.

88. Lint Roller Lampshades: Use a lint roller to quickly clean lampshades.

89. Sparkling Jewellery with Toothpaste: Gently scrub jewellery with toothpaste for added shine.

90. Wipe Down Light Switches: Regularly clean light switches with a disinfectant wipe.

91. Microwave Cleaning with Lemon: Microwave a bowl of water with lemon slices to loosen grime.

92. Deep Clean Oven with Salt: Sprinkle salt on oven spills while hot, then scrub when cool.

93. Lemon for Faucet Shine: Rub faucets with lemon halves for added shine.

94. Vinegar for Shower Head Shine: Attach a bag of vinegar to the showerhead for shine.

95. DIY Glass Cleaner: Mix water, vinegar, and a bit of dish soap for a homemade glass cleaner.

96. Natural Wood Polish: Use olive oil and lemon juice for natural wood polish.

97. DIY Laundry Detergent: Make your laundry detergent with baking soda, washing soda, and soap flakes.

98. Pet Hair Removal with Rubber Gloves: Dampen rubber gloves and run your hands over furniture to remove pet hair.

99. Freshen Kitchen Sink Disposal: Freeze vinegar in ice cube trays and grind in the disposal to clean and deodorize.

100. Freshen Air Vents: Place a dryer sheet on the back of air vents to spread a fresh scent.

Chapter 10: Self-Care Hacks

Welcome to the tenth chapter of "Everyday Life Hacks: Your Guide to Self-Care." In this chapter, we'll explore 100 easy and realistic self-care hacks to help you prioritize your well-being, reduce stress, and find moments of peace and relaxation in your everyday life. These hacks cover various aspects of self-care, from physical health and mental wellness to relaxation and mindfulness techniques. With these hacks, you'll be better equipped to care for yourself and improve your overall quality of life.

1. Start Your Day Mindfully: Begin your day with a few minutes of deep breathing and positive intentions.

2. Stay Hydrated: Drink enough water throughout the day to keep your body and mind hydrated.

3. Prioritize Sleep: Get at least 7-9 hours of sleep each night to support physical and mental health.

4. Practice Gratitude: Keep a gratitude journal to remind yourself of the positive aspects of your life.

5. Take Short Breaks: Regularly step away from work or tasks to stretch and relax your mind.

6. Digital Detox: Schedule time to disconnect from screens and enjoy the real world.

7. Mindful Eating: Savour your meals, paying attention to taste and texture.

8. Set Boundaries: Learn to say "no" when you need to protect your time and energy.

9. Self-Compassion: Be kind to yourself and practice self-compassion in difficult times.

10. Deep Breathing: Use the 4-7-8 breathing technique to calm your nervous system.

11. Connect with Nature: Spend time outdoors, whether it's a walk in the park or gardening.

12. Pamper Yourself: Treat yourself to a spa day at home with a bath, face mask, and relaxation.

13. Active Commute: Walk or bike to work or park farther away to get extra steps in.

14. Positive Affirmations: Use positive self-talk to boost your self-esteem and mind-set.

15. Body Scan Meditation: Practice a body scan meditation to release physical tension.

16. Mini Workouts: Fit short workouts into your day, even if it's just 10 minutes.

17. Hobby Time: Dedicate time to a hobby you enjoy, whether it's painting, knitting, or playing an instrument.

18. Disconnect from Work: Avoid checking work emails or messages after office hours.

19. Social Time: Spend time with friends and loved ones for emotional support.

20. Mindful Walking: Take a mindful walk, paying attention to your surroundings and sensations.

21. Laughter Yoga: Practice laughter yoga to boost your mood and reduce stress.

22. Mental Health Day: Occasionally, take a day off to focus on your mental well-being.

23. Hygge at Home: Create a cosy, hygge environment at home with candles, soft blankets, and warm drinks.

24. Gratitude Walk: Go for a walk and mentally list things you're grateful for.

25. Desk Stretches: Stretch your body at your desk to reduce tension and improve posture.

26. Positive Playlist: Create a playlist of uplifting songs to boost your mood.

27. Grounding Techniques: Use grounding exercises, like the 5-4-3-2-1 sensory check, to reduce anxiety.

28. Positive Reading: Read self-help books or motivational literature for inspiration.

29. Practice Mindfulness: Incorporate mindfulness into daily life, such as during meals or chores.

30. Kind Self-Talk: Treat yourself as you would a friend, with kindness and understanding.

31. Stress Ball: Keep a stress ball or fidget toy at hand to release tension.

32. Set Personal Goals: Work on achieving personal goals, no matter how small they may be.

33. Spa Night: Have a relaxing spa night with facials, baths, and soothing music.

34. Listen to Your Body: Pay attention to your body's signals and rest when needed.

35. Mindful Breathing Apps: Use apps for guided deep breathing and meditation.

36. Me-Time Morning: Dedicate your mornings to self-care activities, like journaling or stretching.

37. Herbal Tea Ritual: Enjoy herbal teas like chamomile or lavender for relaxation.

38. Self-Compassion Breaks: Give yourself mini breaks throughout the day to show self-compassion.

39. Creative Outlets: Express yourself through art, writing, or any creative outlet.

40. Journaling: Write down your thoughts and feelings to gain clarity and reduce stress.

41. Outdoor Exercise: Take your workouts outdoors for fresh air and nature's beauty.

42. Positive Visualization: Visualize your goals and positive outcomes for motivation.

43. Reflect on Achievements: Regularly reflect on your accomplishments, no matter how small.

44. Yoga at Home: Practice yoga at home using online videos or apps.

45. DE clutter Your Space: A tidy environment can help create a sense of calm and control.

46. Nature Sounds: Listen to nature sounds like ocean waves or birdsong for relaxation.

47. Deep Clean and Organize: Tackle a deep cleaning or organization project for a sense of accomplishment.

48. Affirmation Cards: Create or buy affirmation cards to boost your self-esteem.

49. Mindful Showering: Practice mindful showering, paying attention to the sensations.

50. Plant Care: Caring for plants can be therapeutic and provide a sense of accomplishment.

51. Set Realistic Goals: Set achievable goals to prevent feelings of overwhelm.

52. Mindful Cooking: Cook with intention, savouring each step of the process.

53. Self-Reflection Time: Spend time in self-reflection to understand your thoughts and emotions.

54. Digital Sunset: Create a routine of disconnecting from screens an hour before bedtime.

55. Visualization Exercise: Imagine a peaceful place during moments of stress.

56. Warm Lemon Water: Start your day with a warm glass of lemon water for hydration and digestion.

57. Mindful Technology Use: Be conscious of your screen time and its impact on your well-being.

58. Unplug on Weekends: Take a break from technology on weekends to recharge.

59. Spa Bath Bombs: Treat yourself to a spa-like bath with bath bombs and essential oils.

60. Playful Activities: Engage in playful activities to reduce stress, like colouring or playing a game.

61. Positive Morning Routine: Start your day with a positive morning routine, such as affirmations or meditation.

62. Hug a Loved One: Physical touch, like hugs, can release oxytocin, a feel-good hormone.

63. Mindful Eating: Practice mindful eating, savouring each bite and being present at mealtime.

64. Disconnect at Meals: Avoid screens during meals to fully enjoy your food and company.

65. Aromatherapy: Use essential oils or scented candles for relaxation and mood enhancement.

66. Healthy Meal Prep: Prepare healthy meals in advance to save time and nourish your body.

67. Warm Compress: Apply a warm compress to your forehead or neck to relieve tension.

68. Disconnect from Negative Influences: Limit exposure to negative news or people who drain your energy.

69. Music Therapy: Listen to calming or energizing music, depending on your mood.

70. Midday Walk: Take a walk during your lunch break to refresh your mind.

71. Positive Visualization: Visualize your goals and dreams for motivation.

72. Journal of Accomplishments: Keep a journal of your achievements, big and small.

73. Yoga and Stretching: Incorporate yoga or stretching into your daily routine.

74. Disconnect from Work: Avoid work emails and tasks after work hours to unwind.

75. Intuitive Eating: Trust your body's hunger and fullness cues for a healthier relationship with food.

76. Self-Care Date: Schedule regular self-care dates with yourself.

77. Positive Books and Podcasts: Consume content that inspires and uplifts you.

78. Fresh Air Breaks: Step outside for a breath of fresh air to clear your mind.

79. Gratitude Ritual: Express gratitude daily, whether verbally or in writing.

80. Warm Shower before Bed: Take a warm shower before bedtime for relaxation.

81. Progressive Muscle Relaxation: Practice progressive muscle relaxation to release tension.

82. DIY Facials: Treat yourself to a DIY facial with natural ingredients.

83. Guided Meditation: Use guided meditation apps or videos for relaxation.

84. Nature Walks: Go for walks in natural settings to reduce stress.

85. Self-Care Challenge: Set a self-care challenge for yourself, like trying a new activity each week.

86. Mindful Mind-set: Approach life with a mind-set of mindfulness and awareness.

87. Me-Time Weekend Morning: Dedicate weekend mornings to self-care activities.

88. Herbal Bath Soak: Soak in a warm bath with soothing herbs like lavender and chamomile.

89. Power Nap: Take a short nap to recharge and boost productivity.

90. Positive Affirmation Cards: Create or buy affirmation cards for daily encouragement.

91. Disconnect from Social Media: Take breaks from social media to reduce comparison and anxiety.

92. Dancing for Joy: Dance to your favourite music to release endorphins and lift your spirits.

93. Self-Compassion Breaks: Give yourself mini breaks throughout the day to show self-compassion.

94. Light Exercise: Engage in light exercise like stretching or a short yoga session.

95. Stress Ball Squeeze: Use a stress ball or hand exercises to release tension.

96. DE clutter Your Mind: Write down worries or thoughts to clear your mind.

97. Set Personal Boundaries: Protect your time and energy by setting personal boundaries.

98. Spa Foot Soak: Treat your feet to a relaxing foot soak with Epsom salt and essential oils.

99. Disconnect from Negative Influences: Limit exposure to negative news or people who drain your energy.

100. Nature Escape: Plan nature getaways or day trips to rejuvenate your soul.

Don't miss out!

Visit the website below and you can sign up to receive emails whenever PA BOOKS publishes a new book. There's no charge and no obligation.

https://books2read.com/r/B-A-STTAB-PZYPC

BOOKS 2 READ

Connecting independent readers to independent writers.

Also by PA BOOKS

Hogan's Key
Kimberly & the Five Strange Goldfishes
The Enchanted Library
The Misadventures of Pirate Pete
From Wheel To Web: 40 Remarkable Inventions
Once Upon A Sleepy Time
The Global Game - The Evolution Of Football
Strides To Success: A Beginner's Guide to Running
The ChatGPT Handbook
Climate Crossroads
1000 Everyday Life Hacks
Urban Exploration - London The Comprehensive Travel Guide